Dear Parent:

Buckle up! You are about to join your child on a very exciting journey. The destination? Independent reading!

Road to Reading will help you and your child get there. The program offers books at five levels, or Miles, that accompany children from their first attempts at reading to successfully reading on their own. Each Mile is paved with engaging stories and delightful artwork.

Getting Started
For children who know the alphabet and are eager to begin reading
• easy words • fun rhythms • big type • picture clues

Reading With Help
For children who recognize some words and sound out others with help
• short sentences • pattern stories • simple plotlines

Reading On Your Own
For children who are ready to read easy stories by themselves
• longer sentences • more complex plotlines • easy dialogue

First Chapter Books
For children who want to take the plunge into chapter books
• bite-size chapters • short paragraphs • full-color art

Chapter Books
For children who are comfortable reading independently
• longer chapters • occasional black-and-white illustrations

There's no need to hurry through the Miles. Road to Reading is designed without age or grade levels. Children can progress at their own speed, developing confidence and pride in their reading ability no matter what their age or grade.

So sit back and enjoy the ride—every Mile of the way!

For Cleo,
who likes to sleep on my head
M.K.

To my husband Brian and my dog Sally—
thank you for giving me
a warm place to live.
A.H.

Library of Congress Cataloging-in-Publication Data
Knudsen, Michelle.
Cat hat / by Michelle Knudsen ; illustrated by Amanda Haley.
   p.   cm.— (Road to reading. Mile 1)
Summary: A cat looks for the perfect place to take a nap.
ISBN 0-307-26115-8 (pbk) — ISBN 0-307-46115-7 (GB)
[1. Cats—Fiction.] I. Haley, Amanda, ill. II. Title. III. Series.

PZ7.K7835 CAT 2001
[E]—dc21   00-061003

A GOLDEN BOOK • New York
Golden Books Publishing Company, Inc. New York, New York 10106

ISBN: 0-307-26115-8 (pbk)
ISBN: 0-307-46115-7 (GB)

10 9 8 7 6 5 4 3 2 1

Cat Hat

by **Michelle Knudsen**
illustrated by **Amanda Haley**

Ralph is a cat.

He likes to nap.

Ralph needs a cozy spot.

Someplace high.

Someplace warm.

Someplace safe.

Ralph looks around.

Is this a good spot?

No, it's not.

Is this a good spot?

No, it's not.

Is this a good spot?

Yes, it is!

"Is that a hat?"

"Yes–a cat hat!"

Ralph found a good spot.

Someplace high.

Someplace warm.

Someplace safe.

Ralph's a happy cat.

A happy cat hat!